The Depth of Simplicity

Men do not fail commonly for want of knowledge,
but for want of prudence to give wisdom the preference.
What we need to know in any case is very simple.

Henry David Thoreau

Jesús M. Pérez

The 7 Volume Series, Manuel's Notebook: A journey of Self-Discovery

1. A Thousand and One Wise words

2. The World of Words

3. For the Love of God

4. La Siguaraya

5. Dictionary of Terms Related to Writing

6. Lessons from Gurdjieff's Teachings

7. The Depth of Simplicity

Volume 7

The Depth of Simplicity

Title: The Depth of Simplicity

Copyright © Jesús Manuel Pérez 2020

Editor/ Author: Jesús Manuel Pérez

Cover design: Luis Fernando Peralta

Diagraming: Luis Fernando Peralta

ISBN: 978-9945-8-0683-0

1st Edition January, 2020

Acknowledgement

As I write these words to thanks all those who made possible this work, I feel a very strong need to, not just write words as a formality, but to express my most profound gratitude from the bottom of my heart. This work is not another paper of the many I've written; it is the result of a long distillation of many instructions, warnings, and advices that I've been fortunate to receive in my, rather, peculiar and eventful life.

The list of people that I am indebted to is large indeed. To all of them my most sincere gratitude. A special mention goes to the teachings of George I. Gurdjieff's and to those of Baba Muktananda.

Table of Contents

Foreword

Manuel's notebooks are a series of writings made over more than 40 years. Since childhood, I've been fascinated with the idea of documenting whatever crossed my mind. One day, some friends introduced me to George I. Gurdjieff's ideas. Soon, it was evident how easy it is to misunderstand and be misunderstood. This time, the drive to express myself turned into the need to find out everything possible about words. As the investigation yielded promising results, my enthusiasm grew exponentially. Luckily, a close cousin of mine is an expert in the field and, with her help, things began to take shape to the extent of culminating in a book: *The World of Words.*[1] However, several years went by before finishing it. During that time, my daughter Theresa, who saw me spend hours and hours in front of the computer, one evening, unable to refrain herself, exclaimed:

When are you going to finish a book!

Touched on my susceptibility, the question: what to publish? demanded an answer. At that time, the book about words was far from nearing an end, but a project about my collection of aphorisms was practically finished. As a tribute to my father, I had taken upon myself the organizing of a selection of wise words sequentially, so that one led to the other in the style of a narrative. The final result: *2000 and One Wise Words*, turned out to be the natural choice for a first publication.

Over time, the work on *The World of Words* ended and that was the second publication. Meanwhile, in the Gurdjieff groups, I worked hard with the ideas present in the book: *All and everything.*[2] One or another piece of information made me think that reading the Bible could clarify some things, but a strange uneasiness kept me away from the Holy Scriptures. Several attempts to clarify the matter did not work. Nevertheless, stimulated by my new interest, I managed to follow up on the biblical theme, a work which resulted in the book: *For the Love of God.*

---

[1] Published in Spanish as *El mundo de las palabras*, Edición privada, 2009.
[2] George I Gurdjieff, *All and Everything* Two River Press, Aurora, Oregon, 1993.

I continued writing and managed to finish several more books. However, for one reason or another, all the work additional to the first two publications was archived. What I never put aside was my hope of one day sharing all my writings with the public. Today, determined not to postpone it any longer, I made a selection of seven works to start the publications in a series titled: *Manuel's Notebooks, a Journey of Self-Discovery*.

They follow the natural sequence of my writings. The series begins with my two previous publications, but revised, expanded and updated:

The first, *A Thousand and One Wise Words*. The imperishable wisdom of the years expressed in a few words. Really, a pleasant stimulus for everyone's mind.

The second, *The World of Words*, began as a simple desire to learn to communicate and became a determining tool to address my concerns and share the immense amount of experiences accumulated in my hectic life.

The third, *For the love of God*, is a book that emerged from a complex situation. The Catholic formation I received in my childhood placed me in a difficult position. On the one hand, the biblical teachings and on the other, what I observed around me. It took me a long time to clarify what was happening and this work turned out to be a key part of the process.

The fourth, *La Siguaraya*, is a short novel about the amazing events occurring daily in my beloved country, Dominican Republic. Virtually, all of the data in it was taken from local newspapers. Remarkably, despite the chilling nature of the news, they have not caused a reasonable change. It is as if we had become accustomed to the inconceivable. Thus, I chose to dramatize the situation in a novel so that, in some way, the information would remain easily available to present and future generations.

The fifth, *Dictionary of Terms Related to Writing*[3], materialized in a rather unexpected way. It was inside a bookstore where an experience occurred that took me directly to my office and, without stopping, I shaped this instructive and enjoyable book.

The sixth, *Lessons from Gurdjieff's Teachings,* is the result of a long period of studying his work. In it, I present a selection of his teachings arranged in the way that I found most beneficial for my inner search.

The seventh, *The Depth of Simplicity*, as stated in the acknowledgment section of the book:

> This work is not another paper of the many I've written; it is the result of a long distillation of many instructions, warnings, and advices that I've been fortunate to receive in my, rather, peculiar and eventful life.

* * * * * * *

---

[3] Published in Spanish as *Diccionario de términos relacionados con la escritura.*

Introductory Notes

i. Brief Background

> With order and time,
> the secret is found to do everything,
> and to do it well.
>
> Pythagoras

Brought up as a catholic through a difficult childhood, my adolescence turned out to be intense and traumatic emotionally as well as mentally. Uneasy about my state of affair, I checked into everything that came my way: philosophy, literature, the origin of Christianity, the Gnostics, the Indian tradition, the Egyptian Pharaohs, Sufism, even UFOs and the possibility of alien's intervention in our planet among many others subjects.

With such a wide variety of information inside my head, I felt a very strong need to arrange those that most impressed me into a coherent whole. But, all the subjects that caught my attention demanded a great deal of research in order to write anything about them. As I worked my way through any particular issue, inevitably, one thing intermingled with another to an extent that it became difficult to nail down the precise theme of my writing.

Unhappy with the outcome, my life felt in a turmoil that only started to settle down when my path crossed with the Gurdjieff's work. Through the study of his system my questions began to be answered. Later on, to my reassurance, everything I've found useful was reaffirmed with what I learned from Baba Muktananda's teachings.

The new information I had access to allowed me to conceive a sense of totality from which I could depart into the different areas that attracted my interest without losing track of my focus.

The present work contains a selection of topics that I consider critical for understanding reality. Each one of them concentrated on the key points that elucidate the importance of the issue in question.

* * * * * * *

ii. Simplicity

> No matter how complex anything may seem to be,
> its intrinsic simplicity can always be determined.

My uneasiness with what is simple began with the following words:

> To know is to know everything.
> Not to know everything is not to know.
> To know everything one has to know *very little*,
> but to know that *very little*
> one has to know a hell of a lot.
>
> G. I. Gurdjieff

What is this "very little" Mr. Gurdjieff is referring to? Through a lifetime of wondering, many possible answers crossed my way, but there was always something no quite right. Then, I ran into the book *The Miracle of Mindfulness!* by the Vietnamese Zen master, Thich Nhat Hanh, where it is written the following:

Washing the dishes to wash the dishes

While washing the dishes one should only be washing the dishes, which means that while washing the dishes one should be completely aware of the fact that one is washing the dishes.

If while washing the dishes, we think only of the cup of tea that await us, thus hurrying to get the dishes out of the way as if they were a nuisance, then we are not washing the dishes to wash the dishes.

What's more, we are not alive during the time we are washing the dishes. In fact, we are completely incapable of realizing the miracle of life while standing at the sink. If we can't wash the dishes, the chances are we won't be able to drink our tea either. While drinking the cup of tea, we will only be thinking of other things, barely aware of the cup in our hands. Thus, we are sucked away into the future and we are incapable of actually living one minute of life.

*

So, there it is, what could be simpler than washing dishes? And yet, the proper way of doing it requires a something peculiarly difficult that somehow evades our ability to recognize it.

* * * * * *

iii. The Relation Between the Observer and the Observable

Consider the setbacks as an exercise.

The problem of lack of synchronization with the present moment is a critical aspect of the search for truth. In order to harmonize the relation between the observer and what is being observed it is inevitable to determine the nature of each side of the interaction. So, how do we go about this? Certainly, a great deal of pondering, questioning and searching will have to take place. To begin with, it does not matter what turns is given to any data, information, realization, or belief, be it religious, philosophical or of any other possible nature, even if it is a revelation of indeterminate origin, it will always be reduced to what we make out of it. That's it. We are part of a reality that we perceive, whether it is the external or the internal world. These perceptions are what we take into consideration and, with what we can learn from them, we come to conclusions according to our capacity for analysis.

A flight of recognition over the historical data that we have available about the development of our civilization brings out the human capacity to interact with its environment. It just takes a look at our surroundings to realize the extraordinary amount of progress that we, not only enjoy, but that we take for granted such as the pavement through which we walk, vehicles in which we travel, electric light, aqueducts, radio, television, and countless benefits that we have in our daily lives, and every single one of them the result of our ability to observe.

But, how does this relation between the observer and the observable takes place? How is it that there is such an enormous difference in the ability to see from one person to another? There is plenty of reference throughout all the ancient teachings about the need to see reality as it is. The Bible, in particular, has many references to the need of waking up:

How long will you lie down, O sluggard? When will you arise from your sleep?

Proverbs 6:9

*

And when they did not agree with one another, they began leaving after Paul had spoken one parting word:

The Holy Spirit rightly spoke through Isaiah the prophet to your fathers, saying:

Go to this people and say: *You will keep on hearing, but will not understand; and you will keep on seeing, but will not perceive; for the heart of this people has become dull, and with their ears they scarcely hear, and they have closed their eyes; otherwise they might see with their eyes, and hear with ears, and understand with their heart and return, and I would heal them.*

Acts 28:25-27

The most remarkable aspect of this information is that it implies the notion of man being immersed in a world of illusion[4], followed by the inevitable question: if we are not seeing reality as it is then, what is happening with the observer?

* * * * * *

---

[4] Illusion = Misleading mental image provoked by a false perception of reality due to the erroneous interpretation of the data that the senses perceive. https://translate.google.com/?sl=es&tl=en&text=Ilusi%C3%B3n&op=translate.

I. Limited Knowledge

> The truth will set you free,
> but first it will make you miserable.
>
> James A. Garfield[5]

1. For Truth Sake

Ptolemy in the second century BCE, in his work, *The Almagest*, affirmed that the Earth was the center of the Universe and elaborated a complex system of the orbits of the planets. It was not until fourteen centuries later that Copernicus proposed that the Earth and the other planets orbit around the Sun. For a long time, many people accepted as "truth" that the Earth was flat and the list of "truths" that have been reevaluated over time is endless. Regrettably, these assumptions lend themselves to innumerable misunderstandings, disagreements and all kinds of inconveniences that have given rise to, and continue to give rise to, all the wars and all the unnecessary disasters to which human beings have been subjected.

Attachment to beliefs and values based on limited knowledge is like a kind of quicksand in which we sink deeper and deeper until we can no longer function. I remember a television program about deforestation in which one of the people living from the tree cutting business told the defenders of nature that the species that was in danger of extinction was that of the lumberjacks, that why don't they think of saving them. This man completely convinced of his "truth" does not realize that his knowledge is limited to its immediate environment and he has no idea of the consequences of his actions on a larger scale.

In the midst of this state of affairs, those who question themselves about what they are and about the reason for their existence become, in one way or another, seekers of the truth. Seekers of that absolute truth that contrasts with the assumptions that, however significant, belong to the domain of speculation. Remarkably, this search is similar to putting together a puzzle of which we have no idea of the final result, and of which we have had only glimpses of some of the pieces

---

[5] James Abram Garfield was the 20th President of the United States, serving from March 4, 1881, until his assassination later that year.

that compose it. This problematic is represented in a classic story whose origin goes back to ancient India. In it, each one of a group of blind men touches an elephant in a different place to determine what it is. The differences between the tail, fangs, legs and other parts of the animal were so large that the gentlemen could not reach an agreement.

How do you convince someone that, despite his/her truth, there are other things to take into consideration? This opening of the eyes, in which visionaries of all times have insisted, is an ever present challenge and how much we recognize that reality determines the progress we can make in our search for truth.

* * * * * *

2. Do not believe me, make sure what I say is true

> To discuss the legitimacy is not always easy.
> The Buddha insisted strongly on the necessity
> of examining the propositions put forward by Him,
> and of understanding them personally
> before accepting them as true.[6]

Do not believe me, make sure that what I say is true. I heard these words for the first time in the study groups of Gurdjieff's teachings. Then, I found the quote I use as an epigraph on this page. This message confronts us with the ever-present challenge of having to stand on our own feet. The validity and importance of this proposition is obvious. However, for one reason or another, the generalized conditions within daily life are conducive to dependence. An issue that perhaps has its origins in the total helplessness and impotence of the newborn infant. For that reason, or for any other reason, for most human beings to do what they may intend to do, they have to overcome an inertia deeply rooted in their nature. Hence, it is crucial not to yield to the temptation to accept the apparent value of whatever confronts us. Especially, when it is the opinions of others. But, we live in a very complex world where appearances are deceiving and, although we may have arrived at logical conclusions in which we firmly believe, it is very easy to be confused.

So, it is critical to be alert and the only way to be sure of the certainty of any information that concerns the search for the truth is through personal experience: we must directly confirm the truth of everything that concerns us. Interestingly, this activity has a collateral benefit since what is learned in this way becomes part of us: it is not a mere intellectual realization that can easily be forgotten, but an integral part of what we are.

---

[6] Alexandra David-Neel, *The Secret Oral Teachings in Tibetan Buddhist Sects* p. 7 City Light Books, 1981

The Masters of the secret teachings say that the truth learned from another is of no value, and that the only truth which is living and effective, which is of value, is the truth we ourselves discover.

If this were not the case, it would be enough for us to read the innumerable works in which philosophers, savants and doctors of the different religions have explained their view and to choose from among them one which agrees with our own ideas and to which we can cleave. This is what is done by most of these individuals whom the Tibetans classify in the intermediate category of the average-minded.[7]

* * * * * *

---

[7] Alexandra David-Neel, *The Secret Oral Teachings in Tibetan Buddhist Sects* p. 13 City Light Books, 1981

3. The Very Serious Problem of the Different Levels of Understanding

> To believe that one knows
> is the greatest of the barriers which prevent knowledge.
>
> Alexandra David-Neel

A problem that arises immediately in any group of people is that the ability to understand varies from individual to individual. The inevitability of having to live with all kind of people is a great challenge for anyone who is questioning reality and is looking for the truth.

To begin with, the use of the word understand tends to intermingle with that of the word comprehend. In spite of the fact that dictionary definitions give the word comprehend a deeper level of realization than to the word understand, the two terms are commonly used synonymously. However, they are also used with a subtle difference between them. A typical example of this is when one can read a text, but has no idea what it means. In such a case, it is possible to say that one understood the words but did not comprehend the meaning. It can also be valid to express it the other way around, that one comprehended the words but did not understand their meaning.

This issue applies to all form of perception. Any interaction between the observer and the observable has a multidimensional aspect that goes from a simple "face-value" appreciation of the experience into deeper and deeper layers through which we can access more and more information.

It is evident that one thing is to learn how certain things work, to know how to carry out the processes that allow their operation and another, very different, is to put that knowledge into practice and act in a manner consistent with what we have learned. This is clearly verified in any manual work such as mechanics or carpentry where, no matter what theory has been learned, without practical experience, performance is invariably very poor.

* * * * * * *

II. Starting Point

The longest journey
begins with a first step.

Japanese proverb

1. Communication

Since man began to walk on Earth he had to face the imposing nature that surrounded him and which he was forced to understand for obvious reasons, ranging from the imminent need to survive to simple curiosity. The specifics of how man evolved from his first appearance on Earth to the great civilizations he built over time are shrouded in mystery. Regardless of what happened, no progress would have been possible without some form of communication and it is widely accepted that the greatest achievement of humanity is the development of language, first spoken and then written.

*

The development of communication can be separated into three specific periods:

- First, the time in which languages emancipated giving rise to a greater exchange of information, but without writing; it is in this period that oral traditions are established.
- Second, when writing is developed and the writing of stories, anecdotes, teachings... took place without a formal organization.
- Third, the stage in which particular groups of people started to organize those writings to meet their needs.

In the process of gathering and collecting stories told through oral traditions, it was inevitable to be selective as to what to choose to preserve and then organize the information in a way that would accommodate the preferences of those involved in such activities. The least that can be said about this period is that the result has been very complex. The oldest and most influential books are composed of data and stories grouped in ways that give rise to innumerable questions and, as if that wasn't enough, the great limitations of translations are introduced. This situation requires a high degree of prudence in terms of the study, analysis and assimilation of so much material available.

* * * * * * *

2. The Transmission of Knowledge and the Problem of Interpretations

> To reason and to convince, how difficult, long and hard!
> To influence? How easy, fast and cheap!
>
> Santiago Ramón y Cajal

Those who have some data that they consider useful have the possibility of keeping it for themselves or of sharing it. This is not necessarily an option, it can be an inclination or an irresistible drive.

The word *gospel* is used to refer to a particular group of texts (mainly those included in the Bible) but its etymological meaning is simply: good news, preferably of a public nature. So, the original sense of the term is to spread news considered good. Now, one thing is to issue a statement, a message, or express a new idea and another is the interpretation given to what is transmitted.

This situation is fertile ground for speculation. The data of any information lends itself to manipulation, which makes it possible to eliminate or change some of them and thus introduce a series of changes that distort the real meaning of the original text. This is particularly true in translations since the interpretation of the meaning of the terms depends on the ability and intentions of the translator. Over time, new generations, ignorant of the origin of these texts, take their veracity for granted, thus creating a world of misconceptions that can go to radical extremes.

The teachings of the Masters who left nothing written and even those of the numerous Masters whose authentic works we possess have always given rise to interpretation, to developments which, in some cases, have added to and brought out the significance of the original doctrine, and in others have falsified the initial meaning[8].

---

[8] Alexandra David-Neel, *The Secret Oral Teachings in Tibetan Buddhist Sects* p. 7 City Light Books, 1981

In relation to this issue of what is transmitted and what is interpreted, I share the following:

Verbal reasoning is based on experience of words. Formal reasoning –reasoning by forms– in Gurdjieff's meaning is based on experience through the senses.

A man who had read about camels, but never seen one, could enter into a long discussion about camels, but what would his opinion be worth about what one kind of camel or another compared with the man who had raised camels?

In our society both kinds of reason are necessary, since the existence of society depends on people keeping together, and this depends on communication by words which, for this purpose, are symbols; they are like tokens, paper money, in relation to the gold reserve. This paper has a use but no value, or rather, a symbolic value.

Verbal reasoning, like paper currency, is greatly inflated. We ought to be very clear about the merits and defects of verbal reasoning, since so much of what is called education, lecturing, preaching, and popular writing is based on this; it is not backed by actual experience.

A. R. Orage[9]

* * * * * * *

---

[9] Taken from C S Nott, *Teachings of Gurdjieff*, pg. 159 Samuel Weiser, Inc. 1971

3. Common Language

> Poets say great and wise things
> that they themselves do not understand.
>
> Plato

To the extent that we understand our situation, we go on realizing that many things are not clear and that clarifying them requires great efforts. To achieve this, communication requires a common language and, interestingly, that does not refer to the same idiom. A thorough understanding of the terms used is essential for a clear, precise and meaningful exchange that establishes a bridge through which the information desired to be transmitted can flow.

In language, the sense of the relative plays a preponderant role. To understand any term used in communication, one must take into account not only the context in which it is used, but also the epoch, the geography, as well as the social and cultural particularities in which the communication takes place. However, it is possible to establish premises that function as reference points in which the precise meaning of the terms used is specified. Thereafter, the seeker's responsibility is to locate he or herself in relation to the transmitted information. This situation is evident in the following words:

> *He who has ears to hear, let him hear.*
> Mark 4: 9

On the other hand, as Einstein[10] said:

> *We cannot solve our problems*
>
> *with the same level of thought*
>
> *that created them.*
>
> *
>
> *Do not pretend*
>
> *that things are going to change,*
>
> *if we continue doing the same.*
>
> * * * * * *

---

[10] These words are found in Einstein's posters. However, it has been questioned whether he used those exact words or if they are the result of paraphrasing him.

III. Relevant Data

> Many psychic processes can take place only in the dark.
> Even a feeble light of consciousness is enough to change completely the
> character of a process, while it makes many of them altogether impossible.
>
> G. I. Gurdjieff

1. Human Beings

I never thought about what to be human is until a particular news hit me with overwhelming force. Before that moment humans were humans, of course, it was clear that there are good and bad people but it never occurred to me how bad, bad people could be. In a rather average day, I was enjoying a cup of coffee in the company of a very good friend when I found out through a newspaper that a man had raped a two years old girl, killing her in the process. In disbelief, I asked my friend, a neurosurgeon and expert in brain malfunction, how is it possible for a human being to do such a thing. He went on giving me a long explanation about the complexities of the frontal lobule, the billions of neurons in the brain, the elusiveness of the working of consciousness and the narrow link between animals and humans. His words reminded me of a passage from the *Panchatantra*:

> For if there is no mind debating good and ill,
> and if religion send no challenge to the will,
> if only greed be there for some material feast,
> how draw a line between *man-beast and the beast?*[11]

It is evident that the Universe has given rise to an endless number of creatures, each with its potentialities and its limitations. A critical aspect of everything that exists is its interactive nature: Any field of force or any particle is constantly interacting within the medium in which it is found and the more complex the structure, the more activity that can take place.

Unlike the inanimate things, animals are distinguished by their capacity to be aware of their environment, which in turn determines their chances of survival. Moreover, this faculty has a potential for development: it can expand.

[11] Arthur W. Ryder translation of The Panchatantra, p.9 The University of Chicago Press, 1964

Each animal has characteristic of its own and the potential of this ability varies from one creature to another within a wide range of action that is limited only by the body in which it manifests.

Through man, it allows him not only to be aware of the outside world, but also to be aware of himself. However, if this faculty is not cultivated, it remains at its most basic levels. This reality places men within a framework, a sort of transitional zone characterized by its potential for development. Within this operational range, if a man, for whatever reason, does not evolve, then his behavior will not be differentiated from that of an animal, which explains the predatory acts that some people commit, such as the one I read in the newspaper.

This issue of the possibilities of man behavior ranging from an animal to a human level, with a whole world of varieties in between, face us with the reality behind the need to search for the truth, because the work of a seeker is essentially the expansion of his consciousness. We are born at a certain moment and will die for sure at another; what we do in between may not be 100% determined by external factors but it is greatly influenced by them. If we want to go to New York, it is not the same to go there from Montreal than from Miami. Every variable that imposes itself on us like *country of origin, race, physical make-up, religion, social status, economic availability*, etc., has an influence in determining the route through which we have to travel. Obviously, it is different and unique for each individual. This *travel handicap* is the inevitable load that we all have to carry.

* * * * * *

2. Where are we?

> If I see far, is because I am standing
> in the shoulders of giants.
>
> Isaac Newton

Up to the early years of the 20th century, the known universe was circumscribed to our galaxy, the Milky Way. "Then, in the years 1922-23 Edwin Hubble proved conclusively that some nebulae were much too distant to be part of the Milky Way and were, in fact, entire galaxies outside our own".[12] From there on, it has been estimated that there are around one hundred billion stars in our galaxy and that there are about a hundred billion galaxies in the universe.

The most distant object that has been detected is the galaxy MACSO647-JD, which is more than 13 billion lightyears[13] away. It has also been observed that our galaxy, the Milky Way, and the Andromeda galaxy are presently in a collision course. Amazingly, about 96% of the universe is empty space, so much empty space that when two galaxies run into each other there may not be any impacts between the stars and planets, rather what takes place is that they form a larger one.

Despite the extraordinary progress that has been made in the study of the universe, there is nothing to indicate, suggest, or allow to have an accurate idea of the exact magnitude of the universe. Nobody has the slightest idea of what may lie beyond where our most powerful telescopes let us see. To infer and to speculate is all that can be done. However, the following words present a picture of the whole that can be useful:

> Passing to philosophical conclusions, we may say that all worlds must form some, for us incomprehensible and unknown, Whole or One (as an apple is one). This Whole, or One, or All, which may be called the Absolute, or the Independent because, including everything within itself, it is not dependent upon anything, is world for all worlds.

---

[12] This fact was suspected by researchers at least as early as 1755 when Immanuel Kant's *General History of Nature and Theory of the Heavens* appeared. Wikipedia.

[13] A lightyear is the distance that light can travel in one year. Light moves at a velocity of about 300,000 km/sec One light-year is equal to 9,500,000,000,000 kilometers.

The Absolute, that is, the state of things when the All constitutes one Whole is, as it were, the primordial state of things, out of which, by division and differentiation, arises the diversity of the phenomena observed by us.[14]

Well, so it is. Enough for the outside but, what about the inside world? Our thoughts, feelings and the many other inner experiences possible to have provide a very deep and profound world about which we probably know as little as we do of the outside. However, just as with what is out there, inside there are plenty of things to consider and to look into. As a start, let's proceed with the feature of man that most likely has determined the outcome of every event taking place on earth, that is, his beliefs.

* * * * * * *

---

[14] Gurdjieff's words taken from Ouspensky: *In search of the Miraculous*, p 83 Harcourt, Brace & Co. 1949

3. Beliefs

Time uncovers the truth.

Seneca

Beliefs easily lend themselves to being organized under rules and principles that, like columns, support the structure constituted by the ideas that originate them. The elucidation of the way in which these columns are formalized is a vitally important reference to establish the sequence of influences that could have occurred.

Therefore, priority is granted to those of greater antiquity and the oldest sources available belong to the Vedic tradition. The Indians acknowledge that the Vedas are not a single work written by one individual rather, *they were transmitted orally from teacher to disciple; only in later centuries were they committed to writing. For this reason, no real dates can be assigned to them.*[15]

Moreover, the origin of this tradition is a debated issue. On the one hand, the assumption that it originated in the area of Persia and was brought to India by Aryan invaders. On the other, renown scholars argue that those beliefs were in India since time immemorial. Whatever the case, what matters for the purpose of this writing is that there is an ancient teaching whose origins are lost in the past; one way or another, it was taken over by a ruling class for their personal benefits. It must be clear that one thing is the wisdom of ages and the texts written by sages, another what the power possessing beings do with them.

Fortunately, through time, visionaries like Buddha, Jesus and many others stand up against the prevailing nonsense and bring forward the real truth of this ancient wisdom. But, the transmission of this knowledge, inevitably, has to be addressed to different people, in different places, under very different circumstances; no wonder it takes many outward forms as it spreads all over the world, unfortunately, also subject to misuse and abuse of all ssorts. However, above all evil, at the bottom of all of them prevails the seed of truth that blooms every time we give it the opportunity.

---

[15] Clive Johnson, Vedanta an Anthology of Hindu Scripture, p. 9 Harper and Row, 1971

It is worth noticing that the meaning of the terms used to label ancient traditions such as Vedas, Tao, Kabala, Koran all, basically, refer to an ancient wisdom, the receiving, or the telling of such wisdom:

- **Vedas** = Knowledge or wisdom
- **Tao** = The Way
- **Kabala**[16] = Receiving or that which has been received
- **Koran** = The Recitation

Moreover, in India, instead of the term religion, the word Dharma is used which means *the right way of living*. The Vedic texts are packed with instructions of how to conduct our lives, and the same can be said of every religious tradition. Throughout history, humanity has amassed a considerable number of guidelines indicating the proper way for people to live with each other and take good care of their environment. But, of what used is an advice if we pay no heed to it? Words like: *Do to others as you like them do unto you,* should more than suffice to take care of all our problems and yet, in spite of great technological development, we remain as quarrelsome as ever.

* * * * * *

---

[16] Daniel C. Matt, Kabbalah, p.1 Castle Books, 1997

IV. Organized Beliefs

> Sentimentality is deceiving oneself,
> rhetoric is deceiving others.
>
> W. B. Yeats

1. Religion

To study any religion, one must first take into consideration the leader-follower relationship. Unfortunately, there have been many instances where leadership has been based on the ignorance of those being led and not in the knowledge of the leader. Taking the lead does not require great wisdom, but rather a bit of cunning. History is full of examples where really sick people have been able to lead large groups of individuals to commit stupidities and atrocities that challenge the imagination. Without talking about Hitler or Stalin and limiting ourselves to a much lower level, it comes to mind James Warren "Jim" Jones who urged hundreds of his followers not only to take poisoned kool aid, but also to give it to their children; or the case of Marshall Applewhite who persuaded his followers to commit suicide because with the passage of Comet Haley a spaceship was going to pick them up; or that of Charles Manson who incited several young people to commit horrendous crimes and on and on; I could continue to the point of causing nausea to the reader. So, the inevitable question is:

What makes us so surprisingly credulous?

In the oldest settlements tombs have been found in which the corpses are placed in ways that suggest some kind of ritual and the possibility of a belief in life after death. Fear of the supernatural and concern with what might happen after death appear to be determining factors in the ease with which humans are inclined to submit to any apparent power that guarantees them a paradise at the end of earthly life. In addition to whatever natural tendencies there may be, there are several factors that affect the strong inclination of man towards rules, rituals and religions; among them you can consider the following:

1. The imposing manifestations of natural phenomena

In relation to this, there is the widespread belief that thunder, lightning, storms, and the like incited man to conceive the existence of supernatural beings and to consider them responsible for these atmospheric alterations.

2. The stability provided by organization and order

The means available to implement control, invariably, consist of a series of regulations in which stand out rules, commandments, laws, etc.

3. The advantages of power

More control over people and consequently the enjoyment of all the benefits that such a situation brings.

4. The combination of the previous three

They easily converge in the creation and establishment of ceremonies, rituals, festivals and all kinds of activities that serve to constantly validate the established rules.

*

Religion is not in doctrines, in dogmas, nor in intellectual argumentation; it is being and becoming. It is realization.

Swami Vivekananda

* * * * * *

2. Wake-up Call: Gautama Buddha's Revolution

> The Buddha talked about saving all beings from delusion,
> not converting them to a new religion.[17]

As exposed previously, there is an ancient wisdom that has found its way through different channels. It is not clear whether this knowledge is simply transferred from one location to another where it is adapted to their way of living or if different people in different places realized the same thing and developed it according to their possibilities. Regardless of what actually happened, there is an ancient framework that has served as a platform for launching a considerable amount of points of views of the same basic truth. In one way or another, we are all subject to the environment of our upbringing. How we fit under the influence of ours peers depends in our personal needs.

For the sake of having a clear notion of the general situation concerning the different beliefs throughout the world, we can take as a guiding reference the moment in time when the established order imposed by a ruling class was challenged by one who understood the real meaning of life. An event of this nature took place when Gautama Buddha came up with a revolutionary new way of approaching the ancient teaching.

At the time of Buddha's birth, spiritual culture in India was at a low ebb; it consisted wholly in the observance of rituals and sacrifice, for people had forgotten that religion is, primarily, a matter of direct experience.[18]

It must be clarified that the term Buddha in Sanskrit means *enlightened one*; in consequence, it can be applied to anyone who reach that state. The Buddha, whose work gave rise to *Buddhism*, was born in the state of the *Shakya tribe*, in India. For this reason, he is commonly referred to as *Gautama Buddha*, where *Gautama* is the surname of the tribe. It is also appropriate to use the name *Shakyamuni* which literally means: *Sage of the Shakya clan.*[19]

---

[17] Quote #42 from https://ideapodcom/these-55-quotes-from-zen-buddhism-will-open-your-mind/

[18] Swami Prabhavananda, *The Sermon of the Mount According to Vedanta*, p. 45 Mentor Book, 1972

[19] Kogen Misuno, *The Beginnings of Buddhism*, p.210 Kosei Publishing Co. 1981

In a very succinct way, what happened to him is as follows: He abandoned the comfort of his father's house and went through an ordeal of sacrifices living an ascetic life. However, that option was not satisfactory either. Those experiences led him to realize that neither a life of luxury nor one of deprivation were the right way of doing things. While under this predicament, he decided to sit under a tree and meditate until he would reach enlightment, which he did.

There is a story told, either by him or by his disciples, that serves as an analogy to describe how he came to terms with the inadequacy of extremes. In it, it is said that, in one of *Shakyamuni* walks he listened to a guitar teacher advising his students on tuning their instruments not to stretch the strings too much because they could break, but not to let them too loose either because they wouldn't sound well. This is a great example of how an insight can occur to those *who has ears to hear.*

Shakyamuni strongly emphasized that a ruling class of priests is not necessary, that one can achieve self-realization by oneself. In doing so, he created the conditions for innumerable ways to carry out this work. However, he faced an even greater challenge because just telling the Truth to others is not enough. To deal with this problem he adjusted the difficulty of his teaching to the needs and capacities of his audience; an approach called: *Teaching by due course.*[20]

But to what extent does it work? How the one who knows pass on to others his knowledge? How does one deal with incomprehension? This is, in essence, the human drama: knowledge versus ignorance; comprehension versus incomprehension; light against darkness, which brings up the very serious problem of limited knowledge, as the case of the lumberjacks mentioned in a previous chapter.

Don't give that which is holy to the dogs, neither throw your pearls before the pigs, lest perhaps they trample them under their feet, and turn and tear you to pieces.

Matthew 7:6

* * * * * * *

---

[20] Kogen Misuno, *The Beginnings of Buddhism*, pp. 36-37 Kosei Publishing Co. 1981

3. The Gym

> The theoretical understanding of the truth of the Buddha's teachings
> is the first stage toward ultimate enlightment,
> which is attained only after this truth is put in practice.

Among Gautama Buddha's many contributions to helping humanity realize the state it is in, there is one of particular interest: he compared the healing of the mind to the healing of the body.[21] This comparison is very accurate, since they are very similar processes, only that they belong to different operational levels.

In addressing these processes, first of all, there is what is known as preventive medicine on the premises that it is pointless to wait to be sick to take proper care of the body. It is a fact that a well-kept body is less likely to get sick and the same goes for the mind.

For the proper management of the body the ideal situation is to work with a physical trainer. The best results of his work require an acute appreciation of the conditions of the trainees. Inevitably, each of them will have different needs starting with age, since the muscle mass in different stages of life responds differently to the exercises. The variety of demands is, for all practical purposes, infinite. But whatever sequence of exercises is followed, it must be done gradually. For instance, if the goal is to lift 40 pounds and we can only lift 20, we have no alternative but to strengthen our muscles until they are able to lift the 40 pounds. It is obvious that it is not possible to jump from 20 to 40; you have to go through stages: 21, 22, 23 or 25, 30, 35 until reaching 40.

The work with the mind goes through a similar gradual sequence and also has many efforts requirements. Even for simple things as sitting quietly to meditate it is necessary a great deal of discipline. Too much restlessness, too many unnecessary thoughts as well as our animosity interfere with a session intended to be a peaceful one. The parallelism between the two processes goes on and, in both cases, it takes a great

---

[21] Kogen Misuno, *The Beginnings of Buddhism*, p.46

deal of perseverance and commitment in order to succeed in whatever aim we set ourselves to achieve. The big difference is that to find an individual able to guide anyone through the intricacies of inner work is certainly not as easy as finding an adequate physical trainer.

Drawing on very ancient wisdom, Gautama Buddha provided us with a platform from which we can establish a relationship with our potential, and the truth is that no one has added anything to the essence of his teaching; only new techniques or new exercises have been developed to achieve the desired goal. Basically, what is relevant, what is important, what really matters and what is a common denominator in any search for truth is that:

Reality must be seen as it is.

The underlying conception behind all this is that man is created to create himself, that he is created such a being so that he can become something which he is not. But to become what he is not, he has to do certain conscious, intentional work. His being has to grow. This being is also material. Just as our physical bodies need food for their growth and for maintaining their existence, so does the inner being of man require food for its growth and for sustaining its existence.[22]

---

[22] Extract from Pierre Elliot's Inaugural Address to the 1st Basic Course, Claymont Court, 1975

V. All the World's a Stage[23]

> Those in the front are not too far,
> if those in the back run well.

1. The Mountain

From the previous data we gather that the essence of our reality is that we are beings with a potential to develop. There is plenty of information available as to how this development can take place and the climbing of a mountain has been used as an analogy to the challenge confronted by those who seek the truth.

The first issue to determine is whether we acknowledge such a situation and accept that seeking the truth is like climbing a mountain. A person who ignores this or in the event that once given the information do not believe in it, does not concern me. Those that do acknowledge this state of affairs, but by any reason decide not to bother with it, do not concern me either. The group that have my attention is the one that, acknowledging the existence of the mountain, decides to escalate it.

It is within the power of everyone to attain wisdom. Metamorphosis is not sudden, cannot happen from one day to the next; it demands reflection and time, willpower and courage. It can take a lifetime, or many lives, but it is possible; the rest is only a matter of interpretations and paths, the reading of many symbols.[24]

Needless to point out the difficulties most people encounter in reconciling the need to pay the rent with having time for their inner work. The classic approach has been to do one or the other. However, among the caravans going up the mountain, there are others alternatives. There is also another crucial element in the equation: *help from those who know.* Any line of knowledge is subject to a learning process guided by teachers and masters and so on. How do we reconcile our ignorance and our credulousness with the necessary vision to find the proper guidance in order to follow the right path?

* * * * * * *

---

[23] A phrase from William Shakespeare *As You Like It*, Act II, Scene VII
[24] Claude B. Levenson, *Symbols of Tibetan Buddhism*, p.9 Barnes & Noble, Inc. 2003

2. A Peculiar Paradox

> The carnival of the world deceives so much,
> that lives are brief masquerades;
> here we learn to laugh with tears
> and also, to cry with laughter.
>
> Juan de Dios Pesa

There are many exercises that can help us realize the state we are in. The great limitation is that what is aspired to is a conscious realization and, obviously, cannot be achieved unconsciously.[25] So, we are faced with a sort of paradox, that reminds one of the movie *Catch 22* where:

An airman would have to be crazy to fly more missions, and if he were crazy he would be unfit to fly. Yet, if an airman would refuse to fly more missions, this would indicate that he is sane, which would mean that he would be fit to fly the missions.[26]

Indeed, we are faced with a riddle: on the one hand, the need to expand consciousness; on the other, we need a particular amount of it. This situation requires conviction to start working in our search and perseverance to continue working until the result of our work becomes the engine that drives us.

Regardless of what may start our questioning: a powerful experience, a glimpse of the truth, or whatever moves us, the road ahead is full of challenges. Moreover, before we even begin moving forward, there is a considerable amount of work with getting rid of many limiting preconceived notions.

* * * * * *

---

[25] This is a paraphrase of Gurdjieff: In speaking of evolution, it is necessary to understand from the outset that no mechanical evolution is possible. The evolution of man is the evolution of his consciousness And 'consciousness' cannot evolve unconsciously. P O Ouspensky, In Search of the Miraculous p. 65 Harcourt, Brace & Co. 1949
[26] Wikipedia

3. Unnecessary Baggage

> The future tortures us
> and the past chains us.
> That is why the present escapes us.
>
> Gustave Flaubert

In the event that one has the fortune to take sufficient account of the situation as to motivate oneself to undertake the search for the truth, then the challenges begin. As with all enterprises to be carried out, a considerable amount of prior preparation is essential. The conditions where our upbringing takes place are usually not quite favorable for the proper development of our potential. We acquire many misconceptions of how things should be, which plunges us into a world of false values that makes it difficult to see reality as it is.

Therefore, at the very outset of man's pilgrimage through these vast and "scientifically unknown" regions, the reader had best unload all the heavy and useless baggage of educated opinion and scientific dogmas which he may carry. If he doesn't, he will find himself top-heavy, and will capsize or be buried amid the debris of conflicting opinions.[27]

This issue of getting rid of our unnecessary baggage is easier said than done. Just when one may think to be ready, new obstacles of all kinds get on the way. At times, it may seem that some unseen force is intent to make it difficult for us to advance. Questions like: Where do we come from? Where are we going? What are we living for? and so on, must be addressed and they all will eventually boil down to a major key question:

Who Am I?

* * * * * * *

---

[27] Zolar, *The Encyclopedia of Ancient and Forbidden Knowledge*, p. VIII Nash Publishing, 1970

Who am I?

No one can change his situation unless he faces up very deeply to this question of how am I to change, and the question how am I to find a new life, is a real question for him. If you look inside yourself at this moment you can't help but saying to yourself: *But, who is asking this question? Who is this person who is looking for another life?* And you have to be very persistent, very determined to answer this question. You have to really look at it. You cannot accept a readymade answer, but see how it is in reality *Who is this I?* Then you begin to look at the real question: *Who am I?*

At the beginning the answer appears to be very simple. You can say I have an identity. Here is my identity card with my picture in it. It shows a body. A body that eats, transforms energy, lives and dies. It does many other things as well. It has learnt a lot. It has learnt, for example, to speak, as I am speaking now. It can sit in a chair. It is a body that works with its hands and with its feet. We are what Mr. Bennett used to refer to as 'embodied'. We have to face this, first of all: we are all embodied. But, if you ask yourself, do I know my own body, do I know what it can do and what it cannot do, do I know how to use its powers and what are its powers, you will realize that you know very little about your own body.

If you go further and ask yourself: Am I only this body? You will see that the answer is no. I am not only this body, something else exists, thoughts, for instance, exist in me. You look at these thoughts and say: Can I think? Do I think? And if you begin to ask yourself that kind of questions you will realize that your thoughts, most often perhaps your dreams, are only the workings of a quite extraordinary machine, a quite extraordinary mechanism in your brain, which very often you don't even notice and which very, very seldom you can control or direct. So, you begin to see that 'I' is not your thoughts.

When I look at my wishes, desires, likes and dislikes, I see that I am sensitive to some things and not sensitive to others. My state fluctuates, I have a whole life of emotions and feelings which are different from my thoughts, different from by body. I don't know how they arise or where they go; they come and they go. I cannot claim that I made them come. And again, I have to admit that I have no control over them I cannot suddenly feel astonished, or feel sad, or feel joyful. Looking at all this, I begin to see that I am not one. There is a life that goes on in my body, there's a life that goes on in my thoughts, and a third life that goes on in my feelings. So, I have to admit that I know very little about how they affect one another, how they interact with one another. I can even perceive that they don't all pull together.

If I look at this seriously, I begin to admit that I cannot be what I want to be. I cannot act as I wish to act. Again, and again, I find myself doing the things that I don't wish to do. I don't do things that I intend to do. I either fail to do them or even forget all about doing them. I begin to see how little power I have over myself. How little power I have over my life. And I begin to see then why it is so: because I have no 'I', I am not one, I am not connected.

Thus, you can see that just by following the question "who am I?" You will begin to understand some of your practical problems. It is going to be necessary to at least bring together some of these different parts of yourself to see if they can be related in the right sort of way. At least you must have this wish to be one and not many.[28]

* * * * * * *

---

[28] Extract from Pierre Elliot, Inaugural Address to the 4th Basic Course, Claymont Court, September 20th, 1978

VI. Moving Forward

Now is the moment
that never ends.

Deepak Chopra

1. Attention

Many questions to answer and a mountain to climb. In what way does consciousness expand? Certainly, whatever we do, in one way or another, involves attention and the use of the term attention implies the presence of three variables:

1. Who pays attention?

2. What is the attention given to?

3. What allows the relationship between 1 and 2 to occur?

The first two *who* and *what* are relatively easy to determine; but the third: *what allows the observer to observe* is a more elusive matter. If we ask ourselves: what are we realizing in this moment? We face a problem, because many things always surround us and we have a past that, to a large extent, does not pass and a future that has not yet arrived. So, even if we are focused on something, from the moment we question ourselves about what we are doing, the mind flies from one place to another and we can see that our awareness is dispersed, moving around, subject to whatever external or internal stimuli we may be having at the moment.

*

You perceive that you have a certain power over your body. You can make yourself stand or sit If you wish to, you can almost make yourself sit quite still. You can even struggle to some extent with your body. With the help of your body, you can hope to do something. At the same time with your thoughts you have very little power, but you have some power over the direction of your thoughts. So how do you do that, for instance.

One of the means we dispose of, is what we call attention. Attention is something very important which we have to come to understand and which we have to study. It has great power when man is able to use it. It is also capable of great development. When this power of attention is developed in a man, it does enable him to bring a certain order into his life. But our attention as it is now is something we cannot use just as we wish. We begin to see once again that we are not masters of our attention. Other things are our masters. I am walking along the path back to the cottage where I live and I wish to give my attention to a class of movements I shall give that evening. I see one of you passing by. Once my attention is captured by that person, I forget all about my movement class. The moment that person has passed, my eye is caught by the kitchen garden and the weeds growing in it. I begin to feel sorry that there are so many weeds, simply because we have been so slack in our work. Again, I have lost my attention and I am no longer thinking about my movements class. I begin to see that other things have power over my attention. I am not my wish, I am not my will. It begins to be a struggle between what I wish and all the forces that go against it. This is what Mr. Gurdjieff called the struggle of yes and no.

There is the state in which I wish to be and there are all the forces that prevent me from being in that state. Almost everything prevents me; everything I see, everything I think, and everything I do, all these things pull at me, they capture me, they take me away from myself. So, I have to learn to be in myself, that is my struggle.[29]

* * * * * * *

---

[29] Extract from Pierre Elliot, Inaugural Address to the 4th Basic Course, Claymont Court, September 20th, 1978

2. Tools

The attainment of transcendent insight is the real object of the training advocated in the traditional Oral Teaching, which do not consist, as so many imagine, in teaching certain things to the pupil, in revealing to him certain secrets, but rather in showing him the means to learn them and discover them for himself.[30]

*

The previous section faces us with the inevitable question: What relationship do we have with our attention and how much control do we have over it? No doubt that it is of supreme importance to be able to direct our awareness to wherever we want it to go. At this point, we confront a world of possibilities. Fortunately, in relation to this, there is a large amount of information available and easily accessible. As a starter, a simple exercise exposes this reality. Place a clock in front of you and try to keep your attention on the hands; see how much time it takes your mind to get distracted. Insist in trying to keep at it for as little as a minute. Once you manage to see your limitations, then you will have a better idea of what's going on.

With some sense of the order of things established, we can start making decisions about what are our real intentions to carry out the practices that allow the development of our potential. But, it is very important to keep in mind that whether it be prayer, meditation, chanting, studying the teachings in sacred texts or whatever it is within our reach to work with, they are just tools and, like any tool, they are limited to what we do with them. Obviously, some will be more appropriate for one person than for others or some will be better fit for used in one type of work than in others as all tools are, but that does not mean that one tool is better than another, they are simply more or less suitable for the task. Furthermore, tools and hard work by themselves are not enough.

---

[30] Alexandra David-Neel, *The Secret Oral Teachings in Tibetan Buddhist Sects* p.13 City Light Books, 1981

The inevitable reality of needing someone to learn from brings about an aspect of the search that is truly mysterious. The relation teacher-pupil has a nature of dependence where, just as the disciple needs the teacher, the teacher also needs the disciple. A sort of energy move from one to the other in an exchange beneficial for both. Thus, the challenge is not only finding the right teaching, but also to be at a level of deserving the teacher. Moreover, beyond words and any knowledge that could be learned by the seeker there is an energy transfer referred to as *grace*. A very powerful interaction that defy explanation, only the actual experience of it can give us a sense of what we are dealing with.

* * * * * *

3. Afterthought

To examine the people among whom we find ourselves, to investigate the manifold phenomena which continually arise and disappear around us, and then to reach the point at which we can examine the spectator of this spectacle, whom we call "I", that is truly an interesting *programme* which promises unforeseen discoveries.[31]

*

According to the Argentinean singer-songwriter Facundo Cabral:

Good is the majority, but it is not noticeable because it is silent.
A bomb makes more noise than a caress, but for every bomb that destroys,
there are millions of caresses that build life.
The good feeds on itself, evil destroys itself.
The tumor kills you, but dies with you.
(And it does not always kill you, sometimes it wakes you up)
If the bad guys knew what good business it is to be good, they would be good, even if it is
only for business.

* * * * * *

For now, that's all folk. Remember always the advice of the great chefs:

The best recipes are not the difficult ones, the best recipes are always the simple ones.

* * * * * *

---

[31] Alexandra David-Neel, *The Secret Oral Teachings in Tibetan Buddhist Sects* p. 16 City Light Books, 1981

9 789994 580683